# speak beauty

## and kiss
## the
## Son

For
God
so
Loved
the world
That He gave His only Son
That whoever believes in Him
Should
not
perish
but have
Ever
lasting
Life
John 3:16

cheryl sasai ellicott

# speak beauty
## and kiss
## the
## Son

For God so Loved the World That He gave His only Son. That whoever believes in Him Should not perish but have Everlasting Life John 3:16

Sweetwater Still Publishing
Oklahoma, USA

*Speak Beauty and Kiss the Son* © 2022 by Cheryl Sasai Ellicott.

ISBN: 978-1735-6345-6-2
LCCN: 2022941461

Published by
Sweetwater Still Publishing
Colcord, OK

Printed in the United States of America

27 26 25 24 23 22 / 10 9 8 7 6 5 4 3 2 1

To Jesus,

who makes me His song—

# Table of Contents

## A cappella Jubilee

# Honey on my Tongue

# Us Broken

"What I have written,

I have written."

# A cappella

# Jubilee

# Waltz Upon the River

2022

love songs drown
rocket fire
under violent skies
while children dance
sheltered

seeds who die
are born grain
for His embrace
inverts death's kiss
risen

> go—waltz upon the river
> whistle silent tunes
> seize the River's Source
> and never let Him
> Go

## Speak Beauty

2020

On rosy days with honey-sweet middles,
I speak beauty.
I'm smothered in life and good,
Inhaling joy.

On forlorn nights with poisoned centers,
I speak beauty,
Lest I'm swallowed by death of good
And vanish.

My frail tongue chases rainbows and sugar,
And speaks beauty.
Doggedly praising grace and good
In wastelands.

# Lifter of My Head

2016

I see beautiful things.
I hear glorious songs.
The lifter of my head is passing by.

Can I call you Father
When I am alone?
If I follow, will you take me home?

You're the lifter of my head
When this ol' world pulls me down.
You're the refuge for my soul accused;
You're my country, you're my town.

I see beautiful things.
I hear glorious songs.
The lifter of my head is passing by.

Can I call you Father
When I am alone?
If I follow, will you take me home?

I see beautiful things.
I hear glorious songs.
The lifter of my head is passing by.

He's the refuge for my soul accused;
He's my country . . . He's my . . . crown.

# Once Upon a Time

2019

Oh Sweet Spirit
Of Love I know
Your name
    And you are mine.

But I'll never forget
How you found me
Astray
    Once upon a time.

        I had a little faith
        Like a tiny seed;
        Mountains of guilt
        An ocean of need.

        You had a crown of thorns
        And a rugged cross;
        A few sharp nails
        And a fathers' heart.

Now I'm a little tree;
I'm the sheep in your field,
And the man on water
Whose waves have been stilled.

You are a mighty flame
And a rushing wind,
And the cleft in the rock
I'm hiding in.

Oh Sweet Spirit
Of Jesus you gave me
Your life
  And I gave you mine.

May I never forget
That most glorious
Day
  Once upon a time.

# Fire in My Soul

2019

will you wake me up
in the middle of my favorite dream?
will you lift me from
a pit of my own making?

be the fire in my soul
be the reason that it's so
it is finished—I'm forgiven
this I know.

be the fire in my soul
wind of heaven; let it blow
in your mercy and your mighty
name I'll go.

will you write my name
in the Lamb's Book of Life?

and will you carve me, Savior
in the palm of your nail-scarred hand?

you're the fire in my soul
and the reason that it's so
it is finished—I'm forgiven
this I know.

you have made me whole
in your mercy you've filled my soul
so here I testify
on behalf of the Lord Most High:

He's the fire in my soul
He's the reason that it's so
it is finished—I'm forgiven
this I know.

He's the fire in my soul
wind of heaven; let it blow
in His mercy and His
mighty name I'll go.

# Send the Son

2019

You have made all things beautiful.
You do all things well.
Lord your plans for us are glorious,
More than words can tell.

But, oh, sometimes the days are dark
The load seems hard to bear.
The light you planted in our hearts
Wrestles many cares.

Send the sun, Lord. Hear our cry.
When it pours we wonder why.
But while it rains, help us to
Shine, shine, shine.
As we wait on your good time.

Lord you gave your precious Son for us,
God in flesh revealed.

You work all things for the good of those
Whom your love has sealed.

But, oh, you say you're changing us to be-
Come just like your Son.
And won't it take a fire and flood
To get this great work done?

Send the sun, Lord. Hear our cry.
When it storms we wonder why.
But gale or hail help us to
Shine, shine, shine
And to wait on your good time.

Troubles around us, fears within.
We daily crucify our sin.
And when you reign, you make us
Shine, shine, shine.

Bea    uuu    tiful
In your time.

# In the Valley

2018

*Down in the valley, the valley so low*
Where friends and brothers
With me can't go,
There I find you, Lord;
Arms open wide,
Nail pierced hands,
And wounded side.

*Down in the valley, the valley so low*
When I am broken
Only you know.
When I find you, Lord,
There I find rest.
You are my healer.
Oh Lord, I'm blessed.

# Anything For You

2016

If I can go anywhere, I'll go with you.
If I can hide anyplace, I'll hide in you.
If I can do anything, I'll do anything for you.

Lead me through the desert.
You're my cloud and fire.
Take me up the mountain.
You're my one desire

Let me walk on water.
Spring a well of love up from my soul.

If I can sing any song, I'll sing to you.
If I can love any way, I'll love through you.
If I can be anything, I'll be anything for you.

Anything for you.

# Shine Upon Us

2016

On a darkened land your light has shone;
On a silent night your song was sung;
On a thirsty hill your blood was spilled;
On a glorious morn you rose again.

*Let the light of your face*
            *shine upon us.*
*You have filled our hearts*
            *with greater joy.*
*Let the love of your Son*
            *shine through us.*
*And fill our hearts*
            *with greater joy.*

On a shadowed realm your Son has shone;
To a sleeping world His song was sung;
For a pearl in a field His love poured forth.
May the light of His face rise in us!

*Let the light of your face*
                            *shine in us.*
*You have filled our hearts*
                            *with heaven's joy.*
*Let the love of your Son*
                            *shine in us.*
*And fill our hearts*
                            *with your great joy.*

On a lonely stray your grace was shown;
To a silent home your psalms have come;
For a thirsty soul your lifeblood flowed.
On a heavenly morn we'll rise again.

*Let the light of your face*

                            *shine from us.*

*You have filled our hearts*

                            *with lasting joy.*

*Let the love of your Son*

                            *shine through us.*

*And fill our hearts*

                            *with greater joy.*

# Too Wonderful

2019

Are you the Christ
Who stirs up the people?
Are you stirring me?
But you're wonderful.

Are you His Grace
From beyond the curtain?
Holy Promised Child;
Lamb of virgin wool?

Are you the Fire
Who fell from heaven?
You're too wonderful
For the likes of me.

You're too wonderful,
Son of God.

You stopped the sun;
The curtain tore in two.

Fire from heaven fall,
Fall, fall.
Let your glory be
Wonderful
Inside of me.

Wonderful,
Too wonderful.
Jesus you
Are too wonderful.

Fire from heaven fall,
Fall, fall.
Let your glory be
Wonderful

Inside of me.

# Say to my Soul

2019

What do I know?
I know that I want to know
Everything there is to know of you.

What can I say?
I'm yours if you'll have me.
Jesus you are all the world to me.

Say to my soul, *I'M YOUR SALVATION.*
Say to my soul, *COME REST IN ME.*

Sing me a song     that I can't hear, Lord.
Dazzle my eyes     with the unseen.

Tell my poor soul, *I'M YOUR SALVATION.*
Say to my soul, *I AM YOUR KING.*

# My Eyes

2019

He lifted me. He set me free.
He hears me when I cry.
He is the way, the truth, the life.
Jesus is the light.

Trust the Lord
*With all your heart.*
Don't trust your own
*Understanding.*
In all your ways
*Give Him praise.*
He will be your eyes.

His ways are right. His path is straight
He makes the simple wise.
Here am I, Lord. Please lead me.
*Jesus be my eyes.*

# Carry Me Off

2016

swallowed by night
emptied of song
bleakness met light          *You came along*

fearsome and strong
Eternal Son
carried me off          *Carry me off*

come upon me
holy kingdom
in this age          *And the age to come*

overflow me
Holy Spirit
overcome me          *Beautiful One*

# Creation's Hymn

2016

Creation hums through lips of bees,
And songs and dance
Of birds and trees.

Creation sings on ocean waves,
And river currents,
And summer days.

Creation groans and counts to ten
Waiting for Jesus
To come again.

*Maranatha!* His children call.
Bring us home,
Great and small!

# Lord, I Done Done

2015

*I went down to the river to pray,*
*Studying about that good old way,*
*And who shall wear the golden crown.*
*Good Lord, show me the way . . .*

I went down in the river, and I've been reborn;
Into the holy where the veil was torn;
Up from the water like a snow-white dove;
Washed in the precious blood of love!

*I done, done, done—*
*I done what you told me to.*
*By your grace and in your power,*
*I done what I could not do.*

Your days never end, Lord, your ways are right;
Bathe my darkness in your glorious light.
I'm sailin' on mercy, though I earned your ire.
I'll drown my idols in your holy fire!

*I done, done, done—*
*I done what you told me to.*
*By your grace and in your power,*
*I done what I could not do.*

There's a crown a' gold up on top my head;
New life growing from a field of dead.
Crucified with a risen Lord;
Sealed and delivered, I'm the bride adored.

I sing *Hosanna* for the world to see
Sweet Jesus' mystery is Christ in me.
I sing *Hosanna* for the world to see
Sweet Jesus' mystery is Christ in me.

*I went down to the river to pray,*
*Studying about that good old way,*
*And who shall wear the golden crown.*
*Good Lord, show me the way . . .*

# Hundred Proof

2017

Compared to my old Grand-dad,
Granny was a saint.
They called my dad a drifter—but I say he ain't
Gonna stand before the Lord and give
No account for me.
I'm making my own choices,
To bow and bend my knee.

*I need the Holy Spirit —He is my drink of choice!*
*It takes the Living Water to make me raise my voice.*

*My glory hallelujahs may not paint this town,*
*But the fire of revival turned this child around.*

I'm making my own choices,
Giving up my sin.
Owning my own problems—and the state I'm in.
Jesus stood before the Father for
A no-account like me.
Then I started singing the song of Jubilee.

I once was Mama's baby; I was my daddy's child.
Now I am the bride of Christ
—I'm no longer wild.
I'm calling fire from heaven
To burn this baby down.
Use me, Lord, for kindling; shine on this town.

I'm clean. I'm dry. I'm flying high
Standing on His Word.
In the valley or the snowy mountaintop
Soaring like a bird.
Oh, fill my cup with Jesus!
He's my wine and my bread.
My glory hallelujahs
Have the power to raise the dead.

*I need the Holy Spirit —He is my drink of choice!*
*It takes the Living Water to make me raise my voice.*

*I may not see my kin            folk at the pearly gate.*
*But I'm calling upon                        Jesus*

*Before*
*It's too*

*Late.*

# Honey on my Tongue

# The Old, Old Fiddler

2020

*We remember:*

Young lions devoured purple mountains with amber waves
And ancient red giants, above the fruitful plain.
Bulls drank the pilgrim's sweat and rode their golden geese,
And backs of men, crying, Freedom! under spacious skies.
And the fiddler played.

Young lambs woke sleeping pastures, on beautiful feet.
In impassioned self-control, men confirmed their souls,
And lavished precious life, or braved the wilds of thought,
And dignity of motherhood, and every gain divine.
But the fiddler played.

*We concede:*

Old goats chewed the wilderness, for fat and glory-tale,
And selfish gain began to stain the banner of the free.
Young men lingered long and gazed upon the sparkle.
And pretty girls cried, Freedom! and danced on blueberry hill,
While the fiddler played.

Laughing silver birds, in apple pie trees, snared the eagle
And beat the glory back with their charms,
So women in red skirts and men who stumble
Could shuffle on the corner stones with Mom,
As the fiddler played.

*We confess:*

Moreover, they built ivory houses in their alabaster cities,
Despite human tears. And men marched off
While ladies burned their . . . aprons,
And fiddlers fiddled valiantly, with liberty in law,
And played on.

When there came a great hush, the prophet rumbled.
Dense white smoke drifted up, or down;
They couldn't tell for the trees. So they planted more trees
In the soil of the unborn and the pure.
Oh, how the fiddler played!

*We lament:*

Then in dark the lion roared, but no one trembled.
Sweet blue flames licked the columns of the porch
And it fell with a *whoosh!* despite grace shed from sea to sea.
And they took up Nero's song, at the trumpet's call.
Alas, they fiddled.

# Ode to Decency

2020

Row on row filing in
They line the benches stony-faced.
One by one they praise the soul,
Departed now, of Decency.
A kinder gent you couldn't find,
Weeps the man with wrinkled brow;
No mean bones, nor raised his voice,
Echo matrons frightfully.
But oh the boys who line the back
Whisper into fists clenched tight,
And she in black stares ahead,
Shakes her head and sighs aloud.
Nonsense, she mutters. Nonsense.
At last the sappy, syrup speech slows
And stills and cedes to hush
Till only she who loved him well
Is left to speak and left to tell.
Listen, she utters. Listen.
You knew him not, this Decency.
Kind, perhaps, but Decency
Scrapped all day and then some more,
To bring high morals to his shore.
With holy shame and seething wrath
His hate of sloth is legend now;
His feud with lust a bloody war.

Why rumor says, and I agree,
He goodly slew his dark old man,
And kept him down with iron will,
Virtue, mettle, and further still
Through selfless love and hate of vice,
He put himself beneath that knife
To buy the peace by which you slept—Decently.
Decent men and decent folk
Are not born but rather yoked
To love of law and order, still—
And yes it goes against the will,
For all of us, and each of you,
Were born to fail as much as crawl—
There is a way, and a call,
To die to self and give one's all—for the sake of Decency.
Mere babes in arms perceive the time
And understand the need to hold,
To what is good and hate the wrong,
Give Decency more than song!
But if you gather, flower strewn,
And send this good man on his way,
Boys in back and worthless clods
Will play with babes and seize the day.
For love of peace, by which you sleep,
Decency must not stay
Beneath men's feet, beside the way
For even now his blood cries out:
You stony-faced and frightened ones,
Praise my virtue, don your black,
But die with me—to bring me back!

# For Want of a Robe

2020

I knew a blind man
In the region of madmen
Who cherished self-pity and vice.
He called virtue a fabled mirage
And tempered his heart from within.

I met a bleak child
From the land of baldness,
Where hands of the fathers hang limp.
Dressed in virtue, by way of her birth,
She lived in the ashes of sin.

I saw a gaunt bride
Of the country of fatness
Whose gown of honor was soiled.
Virtue's price was far too steep—
It was sold for a sip of gin.

I once heard a man
Tell of more than a man
Who opened the eyes of the bald.
Virtue His robe was drenched in blood
But it never lost its shine.

He sat a new donkey;
He'll return on a horse
For she who wears His robe.
He shouldered a cross and offered virtue
To filthy, bleak, and blind.

#  Kiss the Son

2016

Red sky in the morning;
Sailing on toward night.
Failing to take warning;
Seeing without sight.
Jonah's clue is risen
    —read the Oracle of times.

Nations deep in guile;
Wailers weep in vain.
Sailors of the vile
*Hating on* The Name.
Anchors up to Zion
    —can you read the times?

   *Come on out, God's people.*
  *Share her sins,*
*You'll share her plagues.*
    *Sail away, His people,*
    *To the Ancient of Days.*

*Climb up His Holy mountain.*
*Bow down and kiss The Son.*

Mercy will be given
in The Name of The One.
Climb up His Holy mountain.
Bow down and kiss The Son.

# Us Broken

EARLY POEMS

# Blind Men Dance

2013

they say anger builds, then boils
uncapped radiators blow
searing those who still
                    care

they say                    things
sometimes I                 agree
I'm blown


anger is a dog, puking on my rug
stink leaves a stain
I can't dance alone

                    purging

I see                       things
sometimes I                 join
I'm stained

his dog; my rug
capped in mute stew
rage eats me too
                    numb


we hear                    things
through a                  haze
I'm stewed


he can't see; I should care
unstrung dogs bite
I'm           us      yesterday     dancing

                    boiling       blowing
              puking       stinking
                    purging      staining
              raging       stewing
                    biting       dancing
praying
praying
praying      caring
       healing

The following undated poems
were all written sometime prior to 2000.

# Haze

Dust in my eyes
Brought me here.
I lounge in the crooked chair.
Mist in my head
Lost my mind
Somewhere in the air.

Ghost in the book
Bring me back
Breathe on me for your Son.
Fall from the chair
Onto my face.

It's finished; it is done.

# Deep Blue

On just another low day,
Day of the dragging sole,
I tossed on my bed in rumpled hair,
Took a swim in the favorite hole.

Lucifer was down there,
With his smoke and mirrors too.
I called myself an ocean
Because I was deep blue.

The deeper I swam,
The bigger I was.
My soul was a boundless dream,
Till I drowned in myself
For I was alone.
No one heard me scream.

# Wondering Mood

I've wondered long,
In my wondering mood,
If life is more
Than I've understood.

When things are clear
Like never before
I ask myself,
Have I found a door?

When thoughts are feelings
And truth tastes sweet
I shut my eyes,
Vow no retreat.

But this one thing
I know is true:
If it's gone
I'll not know I knew.

# Arrogance

deep thoughts                  swollen mind
ring my bell
mask of poise
flapping lips                   impart pure noise

should you look                (had you eyes)
what you'd see
I would despise
what you'd hear                more like cries

or squeals                     and I
self deluded lie
wallowing
in the topsoil                 of wisdom

# Outburst

rock the boat; my tempest was
as gentle as a lamb
slay the goat; he knew me for
the starling that I am

roses, roses! wails the silly bird
on the wall
catch me! catch me! foolish girl
closed eyes watch me fall

trouble brewing, storm doing
damage to my soul
anger chewing, madness ruin
outburst takes a toll

# Sugar

Should the wings of the night
Carry me
Till your side's an empty grave
Would you, Oh man,
Bury me,
Or hold on to all I gave?

And what of the day? Should it
Call to me
To wander from my place
Would you beat your arms
For letting go,
Or madly seek my face?

Contemplate my question,      Love,
For this is what I dream:
Am I sugar in your coffee      now?
Or the sunlight's every beam?

## *Vow*

take me in to
yesterday, today, and forever
on a wind like grace
with a smiling face
hold me

hold me up to
somewhere, nowhere, everyplace
with hands like stone
made of my bone
keep me

keep me down to
one truth, two souls, and a trinity
in a whispered shout
what it's all about
kiss me

*This is the oldest one of my poems that's still around.*

# Yes, I Know

1989

Yes I know
The wicked lie in wait
For the righteous.
Lord I know
The enemy seeks my life.

But I will rejoice,
For I know you'll never
Leave me under his power,
And you will
Not let me be condemned.

> *Lord the road you walked, it wasn't easy.*
> *The cup you drank,*
> *Was meant for me.*

> *Jesus take my hand and I will follow*
> *Through the camp of*
> *Your enemy.*

Yes I know
There are trials on the path
Of the righteous.
But I know
There's joy in all my troubles.

And I will rejoice,
For I know you'll never
Leave me under their power.
When it's done
You'll bring me forth as gold.

*Jesus didn't say it would be easy.*
*Just that He'd keep me,*
*And never leave me.*

*Jesus take my hand and I will follow*
*Through the camp of*
*Your enemy.*

I wrote this shortly after my daughter died of cancer
and my young husband lost his faith, hope & direction.
It took him 18 years to find it. But meanwhile,
Jesus remained faithful and true.
Cling tightly to His hand.
-- Cheryl

# Your Poems

ABOUT THE AUTHOR

Cheryl Sasai Ellicott is a wife, mother, grand-mother, artist, writer, editor, and ghostwriter whose life passion is to know Jesus and make Him known.

Born in Washington state and raised in rural Alaska, Cheryl has been married since 1988. She and her husband Mike are veteran homeschoolers, foster and adoptive parents, worship leaders, Bible teachers, and are involved in missions globally.

CPSIA information can be obtained
at www.ICGtesting.com
Printed in the USA
BVHW042257090822
644223BV00003B/24

9 781735 634562